D1415056

Alan
Apostrophe

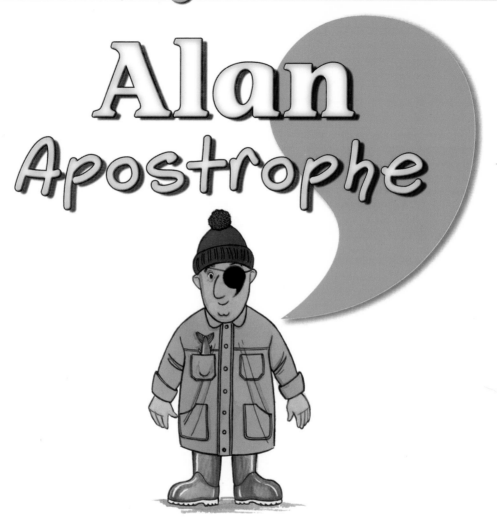

Written by Barbara Cooper
Illustrated by Maggie Raynor

GARETH**STEVENS**
PUBLISHING
A World Almanac Education Group Company

Please visit our web site at: www.garethstevens.com
For a free color catalog describing Gareth Stevens Publishing's
list of high-quality books and multimedia programs, call
1-800-542-2595 (USA) or 1-800-387-3178 (Canada).
Gareth Stevens Publishing's fax: (414) 332-3567.

Library of Congress Cataloging-in-Publication Data

Cooper, Barbara, 1929-
    [Alec Apostrophe]
    Alan Apostrophe / written by Barbara Cooper; illustrated by Maggie
Raynor. — North American ed.
        p. cm. — (Meet the Puncs: A remarkable punctuation family)
    Summary: Introduces the use of the apostrophe through the story of Alan,
a member of the Punc family known as the one-eyed Punc because he wears
an eye patch.
        ISBN 0-8368-4223-5 (lib. bdg.)
        [1. Apostrophe—Fiction. 2. English language—Punctuation—Fiction.]
    I. Raynor, Maggie, 1946- , ill. II. Title.
PZ7.C78467Al   2004
[E]—dc22   2004045322

This edition first published in 2005 by
Gareth Stevens Publishing
A World Almanac Education Group Company
330 West Olive Street, Suite 100
Milwaukee, Wisconsin 53212 USA

Designed and produced by Allegra Publishing Ltd., London
Gareth Stevens editor: Dorothy L. Gibbs
Gareth Stevens art direction: Tammy West

Printed in the United States of America

1 2 3 4 5 6 7 8 9 08 07 06 05 04

Cap'n Alan Apostrophe

is called the "one-eyed" Punc because he wears a black patch over one eye.

He's also known as the Wanderin' Punc because he pops up all over the place, cuttin' down and shortenin' words.

I'm a salty ol' Punc!

3

Cap'n Alan's the skipper of what he calls a fishin' boat. He's brave and he's kind, but he's easily upset when he feels that people are "treatin' 'im 'urtfully," just because he garbles and slurs some of his words.

During Alan's first week at school, his teacher, Miss O'Puncley, noticed that he was squinting.

"Oh, dear," she thought, "he'll have difficulty with his lessons. I'd better talk to his parents."

I'll make an appointment.

Alan's mother wasn't surprised, because she'd noticed that he often looked at her cross-eyed.

She said to her husband, "We'd better take Alan to see Dr. Gaze."

?!"—,
,?•—!"
.!…—*
…. ,?,"
* •!— ,"""
?*—!…. ,—
!?.—*…. !,,.

The very next day, Alan found himself at Puncspec's, where Dr. Gaze, who is an optometrist, tested his eyes.

"Alan's got a vision problem called 'lazy eye,'" said Dr. Gaze. "He'll have to wear a patch over his good eye. It'll make his lazy eye work properly."

Dr. Gaze fitted a pink patch around Alan's head.

With the patch on, Alan couldn't read very easily. He wasn't able to write very well, either. Before long, he'd started speaking poorly, dropping his g's and his h's and turning two words into one.

But Alan wasn't too bothered by his reading and writing problems because . . .

he was brilliant at what
he called 'urdlin' and
pole vaultin'.

Every summer, Alan's father, Aristotle, who was Greek, and his mother, Annie, who was Scottish, would take him to visit relatives. One year, they'd stay with the Apostrophes on the Greek island of Apos. The next year, they'd visit Annie's family, the MacPuncs, on the Scottish coast.

Alan's favorite summer pastime was what he called shell-collectin'.

The Apostrophes
of Apos (don't
ever call them the
Apostrophe's!) didn't
have a lot of money, but
they'd worked hard and
built themselves a fishing
boat — named Cyclops.

Alan's favorite game was
sitting in the crow's nest
with a telescope, looking
out for pirates.

When Alan and his parents stayed with the MacPuncs (be sure you don't call them the MacPunc's!), they didn't spend much time doing what Alan called "messin' around with boats." Instead, they'd put on tam o' shanters and waders and go, as Alan said, "salmon fishin'."

You're probably wondering, however, what happened with Alan's eyesight.

Well, one morning, he rushed into his parents' bedroom and told them that "'e'd been lookin' at 'imself in the mirror, and 'e'd noticed that 'e wasn't squintin' anymore. Dr. Gaze's patch had done the trick, indeed!

Cap'n Athos Apostrophe

You'd have thought that Alan would've been glad to be without his patch, but after several days, he'd started to miss it. Then and there, Alan made up his mind that, when he was older, he'd go to sea and wear a patch like his great-grandfather, Cap'n Athos Apostrophe, who was also known as Black-eye the Punc, a notorious pirate.

The sea was in Alan's blood, so it wasn't long before he'd left home, put on a black eye patch, and gotten himself a job on a fishing boat.

"I'll do anythin'," he said, "mendin' nets, sewin' sails, cleanin' fish."

He'd work day and night, saving all his money to buy his own boat.

"I'm goin' to call 'er 'oratio Nelson," he said.

Alan's crew were two local boys who he called 'enry and 'erbert. While Alan was at the wheel, they'd be flinging out nets and hauling in fish. Appie, the ship's cat, was always nearby, watching.

"What's in the nets, today?" Alan would ask, as he peered at the " 'eaps of wrigglin' 'errin' and 'addock" piled up on the deck.

Alan's Band o' Brothers

Alan now has a bigger boat, called The Jolly Punc, and, as you'll have guessed, he has a bigger crew, too.

"I 'and-picked 'em at the Puncport pier," said Alan. "They're a mixed bunch, but we've got a very 'appy ship."

When you're puttin' in apostrophes,

don't be as careless as Alan is about droppin' letters, the way 'e (he) drops 'is (his) g's and h's, and don't use apostrophes where they don't belong. Alan gets angry when he sees himself in words that mean "more than one" (plurals), such as noisy parrot's and slippery eel's. So, please, keep a careful eye on Alan's apostrophes!

Alan's Checklist

- **Apostrophes take the place of missing letters. Put in an apostrophe where the missing letter would be:**
  I'm (I am)   he'll (he will)
  who's (who is)   didn't (did not)
  can't (cannot)   it's (it is)
  would've (would have)

- **Use apostrophes to form belonging words (possessives), adding "'s" to singular words** (The pirate's parrot), **even if a word ends in an "s"** (Athos's eyepatch), **and adding an apostrophe, only, to plural words that already end in "s"** (The pirates' parrots) **or "'s" to plural words that do not end in "s"** (The crew's boat).

- **To show that something belongs to more than one person, add "'s" only to the last name:**
  Aristotle and Annie's cat.

- **Some names have an apostrophe in them:**
  Miss O'Puncley (last names)
  Puncspec's (business names)
  tam o' shanter (names of things)

- **An apostrophe is used in a date when some of the numbers have been left out:**
  '60 (1960)

- **An apostrophe is also used when writing the time of day in words:**
  It's 9 o'clock in the morning.
  ("o'" is short for "of the")

- **Remember:** Never use an apostrophe in the belonging (possessive) word "its."
  (Alan's boat is on its way.)